TINYWORDS

Issue 10.2

Summer 2010

tinywords 10.2: Summer, 2010

This issue was originally published on tinywords.com from July 6 to September 22, 2010, and is archived at http://tinywords.com/category/issue-10-2/

Editor and publisher: d. f. tweney

Assistant editors: John Emil Vincent, Shae Davidson

Previous publication credits, where applicable, are listed at the end of this book.

ISSN 2157-5010

ISBN 978-0-557-74594-4

sunrise—
all at once
birds leap from the water

—*Deborah Finkelstein*

free from school
the chalk dances
across the sidewalk

—*Peg Duthie*

summer at last
I blow away a grey hair
from my keyboard

—*Fred Flohr*

thick stump
an ant crosses the growth rings
into my childhood

—*Rafal Zabratynski*

new moon
last year's kite
slumped in the corner

—*Helen Buckingham*

museum hall
children study
their echoes

—*Bouwe Brouwer*

fading tattoos
he hauls her wheelchair
from the beach

—*David Serjeant*

Tanka

the voice
of a wrong number
for a moment
wishing I was the daughter
she's trying to reach

—*Kathe L. Palka*

old pond—
a crab sneaking into
the sunken sneaker

—*Helga Härle*

leaf shadows
spatter my skin
this heat

—*Ann K. Schwader*

gnarled banksias
entwined like old lovers
along the track...
how many years now
have we been together?

—*Barbara A Taylor*

wood's edge—
stepping inside
the sound of river

—PETER NEWTON

mockingbird an octave shy of the moon

—*Billie Dee*

war ruins...
suddenly the cicadas
stop

—*David Serjeant*

Cigarette smoke
curls against
the white moon.

—*Chris Moran*

father-daughter talk
my fishing lure
caught in the moon

—*Aubrie Cox*

something less
than the speed of light
camellia blossoms

—*Matthew M. Cariello*

the junkyard crane
grabs another car—
wind-tossed poppies

—*Tanya McDonald*

laundry in the garden
the colorful dresses
full of butterflies

—*Małgorzata Miksiewicz*

rising from prayer

i find myself

in tourist photographs

—karasu / Ross Clark

a row of white houses
across the bay
the glint of binoculars

—*Mark Koerber*

bush track and mountains
all I can see
is one horse fly

—*Duncan Richardson*

between roots
a woodchuck
gathering sun

—*Michele L. Harvey*

a beach day like any other
until she unwinds
the ties of her bikini

—*Scott Duke Kominers*

The sky darkens

The ocean replies

—*Katherine Scott*

Falling rain,
the priest kneels before an empty altar.

—*Jon Summers*

a solitary bird calls to the space between lightning and
thunder

—*ANGIE WERREN*

my colleague
flirting with the workmen
... endless summer rain

—*David Serjeant*

rain in the puddle—
I have nothing to give
to the street musicians

—*Valeria Simonova-Cecon*

towpath—
a blue heron shifts
the twilight

(for Lenard D. Moore)

—ROBERTA BEARY

gone
with the storm
the wind chimes
my neighbors quarrel
deep into the night

—*Barry Goodmann*

seaside rest home
the gentle swell
of his belly

—*Bouwe Brouwer*

over my thoughts the hush of pines

—*Peter Newton*

Her last summer
each day brings
a new flower

—*Michelle Sanders*

workday's end
a construction worker pees
into the summer sun

—*Dietmar Tauchner*

cobwebs
fill the curve
of the snow shovel

—*Bill Waters*

dropping my dog off
at the kennel her whine
amid all the barks

—*Kathe L. Palka*

after the hurricane
only the moon

—*C. P. Harrison*

last day of vacation—
the blackberries
won't let me go

—*Alexa Selph*

cloudy day
I wave at the neighbors
I don't know

—*Joanne Morcom*

a spider
on the floor tile—
checkmate

—*Melinda B. Hipple*

daughter and
mother the
same hard face

—*David Serjeant*

bus stop
an empty bench
and a bag lunch

—*Sue Burke*

from pampas grass
a dragonfly emerges
thunderclaps

—*Joanne Morcom*

gusty wind
chasing one another
three plastic cups

—*Roman Lyakhovetsky*

beach party
the last drop of sunlight
caught in a glass

—*Barry Goodmann*

rain
curtain
of absences

—*Joseph Quinton*

the little spider
hunches sideways—
night shift

—*Melinda B. Hipple*

whispering grass ~
the scythe's sound against
the stone

—*Dana-Maria Onica*

World Series
another layer of paint
flakes off the fence

—*Patricia Benedict*

summer's end
lilies pointing
toward earth

—*Patrick M. Pilarski*

collecting stones
from the river
where I was baptized
moonlight
washes over me

—*Aubrie Cox*

summer's end—
rearranging gravel
in the Zen garden

—*Carol Raisfeld*

last bloom—
closing
the shears

—*Claudette Russell*

Editor's Note

Both the quantity and quality of work submitted for this issue were astonishing. Over a 15-day period, we received 875 submissions, including poems, haiga and haibun.

Selecting three months' worth of daily poems from that incredible pool was really difficult—not just because of the volume, but because we had to say no to many terrific poems. If your work didn't find its way into this issue, please rest assured that's not necessarily a judgment on its quality, even in the editors' own admittedly idiosyncratic estimation.

I hope you enjoy the selection, and this presentation.

Notes on the Poems

page 1, "sunrise..." Previous publication in *Bear Creek Haiku*, Autumn 2008.

page 7, "fading tattoos..." Originally published in *Presence.*

page 8, "Tanka" Previously published in *Ribbons* Vol. 5 No. 3.

page 12, “wood's edge...” Honorable Mention in Kaji Aso Studio 2010 Haiku Contest (Boston, Massachusetts).

page 13, “mockingbird...” Previously published in *Roadrunner Haiku Journal* IX:2.

page 14, “war ruins...” Author’s note: The photo was taken (and the haiku was composed) in a bombed out hotel complex on the Croatian coast last year.

page 25, “the sky darkens...” This poem is included in a hand-bound, self-published book called “Driftwords: Tiny Poems for the Ocean.”

page 27, “a solitary bird...” First appeared on twitter.

page 28, “my colleague...” Originally published in *Riverbed.*

page 30, “towpath...” Previous publications: miniwords 2008 haiku contest 3rd place; Haiku Poets Central Maryland 2008 poemsheet ‘lunch break.’

page 37, “dropping my dog off...” First published in the Australian journal *paper wasp*, autumn, 2009.

tinywords publishes each issue serially, one poem per weekday, at http://tinywords.com. The poems in this issue are also readable online, along with responses by readers, at the following URL: http://tinywords.com/category/issue-10-2/

www.ingramcontent.com/pod-product-compliance
Ingram Content Group UK Ltd.
Pitfield, Milton Keynes, MK11 3LW, UK
UKHW020232250726
13967UKWH00001B/323